When Muslim Teens
rebel

Causes and Solutions

Dr. Mohamed R. Beshir

amana publications

First Edition 2008A.C./1429A.H.

Copyright © 2008A.C./1429 A.H.

amana publications
10710 Tucker Street
Beltsville, MD 20705-2223 USA
Tel: (301) 595-5999
Fax: (301) 595-5888

Email: amana@igprinting.com
Website: amana-publications.com

Library of Congress Cataloging-in-Publication Data

Beshir, Mohamed Rida.
  When Muslim teens rebel : causes and solutions / Mohamed R. Beshir.
      p. cm.
  Includes bibliographical references.
  ISBN 978-1-59008-055-9
  1. Child rearing–Religious aspects–Islam. 2. Parenting–Religious aspects-
-Islam. 3. Muslim youth–Conduct of life. 4. Muslim youth–Religious life.
I. Title.
  HQ769.3.B48 2008
  297.5'77–dc22

                                            2008036863

Printed in the United States of America
by International Graphics
10710 Tucker Street
Beltsville, MD 20705-2223
Tel: (301) 595-5999
 Fax: (301) 595-5888

Acknowledgements

J ust as it takes a village to raise a child, it also takes a family to write a book. And for that reason, I would like to thank my dear daughters for all their invaluable input at the various stages of development of this little book. Hoda, thank you for your motivation, insight, and important contributions when this project was still being transformed from an article into a book. Sumaiya, thank you for picking up where Hoda left off and continuing the journey with me. And Noha, thank you, as always, for your quick and efficient editing skills. It was a pleasure working with such a loving and devoted team to bring you this book. We hope you enjoy it and benefit from it. It may be little, but we pray that it will have big effects insha Allah.

Mohamed Rida Beshir

Contents

How This Book Came To Be

O ne of the most wonderful words of wisdom by Ali Ibn Aby Taleb RAA is: "Raise your children using different ways than those that were used with you because they were created for different times and different challenges."[1] A great majority of Muslim parents have failed to understand this insight when dealing with their teens, particularly in North America. This failure has contributed negatively to widening the communication, cultural, and relationship gap between parents and teens. Coupled with a very strong popular teen culture promoting completely different values than the values Muslim parents want to instill in their teens, it constitutes a recipe for disaster for Muslim teens and their parents. That may explain why, without doubt, the most important issue and concern parents have in North America is raising non-troubled teens.

This book is based on an article written by the author that was published in *Americas Muslim Magazine*.[2] The title of the article is "*What is going on with my teenager and how do I fix it? The causes and solutions of teen rebellion.*" We received many positive comments on the article as well as requests to expand on the various topics it covered. The magazine readers felt that due to the space limit imposed on the article, the author had to cut short some of his ideas and thoughts about this very important topic of Muslim teen rebellion, and we think they were correct in their assessment. This is one of the main reasons we decided to expand the article to cover all relevant points of the subject in order to provide full benefits to readers. As such we decided to make the information available in a book format which will give us the opportunity to cover all pertinent aspects of the topic.

1. Mohammad Gawad, *Al-Imam Ali* encyclopedia, Volume 1, *Dar Al-Tayar Al-Jadded*
2. *Americas Muslim Family*, spring 2008 issue

How this book came to be

In this book we will try to provide a positive contribution to help parents save their teens from the negative impact of popular teen culture and succeed in raising them as strong, confident personalities who can contribute positively to their community and to the North American society at large.

In this book, we will start by explaining what we mean by rebellion, and discussing if it is inevitable in the life of a Muslim Teen. Then we will cover three basic ideas. The first idea deals with the causes of teen rebellion in general and additional factors that contribute to Muslim teen rebellion in particular. The second main idea covers the signs of this rebellion and how it manifests itself in the behaviour of our teens. The third and most important part of the book will deal with a comprehensive solution consisting of three components, the most significant of which is the Prophet's SAAW example in dealing with youth, then the role that parents can play complemented with the community's involvement.

We believe that if these components are fully in place, we would see a tremendous decline in teens' tendency to rebel against certain norms and attitudes practiced by their parents as well as other adults in the life of the teen such as community members, Islamic center and mosque officials, and school teachers.

It is important here to note that the cooperation of parents and community members in general and Muslim institutions (such as Islamic centers, mosques, national and local Muslim organizations) in particular is a must to succeed in helping to reduce the phenomena of Muslim teen rebellion. Parents' involvement in ensuring that local mosques and Islamic centers offer effective and attractive youth activities is a must to help our teens utilize their time properly and engage in useful and positive projects that will benefit the development of their personality. Not only this, but parents must also take the initiative to start such activities and projects in their mosques and Islamic Centers. Whenever certain actions are needed, parents should not wait for institutions to initiate these actions on their own. Concerned parents should form committees to look at alternatives and propose solutions to officials in their centers. They should also be willing to put the time and effort required to help make sure that these initiatives are being implemented and become a reality. Most of our Muslim communities in North America are still young and their work is mainly based on volunteers. Parents should volunteer their talents, among other things, to make sure that activities are planned and executed properly. After all they are the main beneficiaries of such projects.

It is our hope that, insha'a Allah, the proposed comprehensive solution in this book will be of great benefit to various communities in general and to our teens and youth in particular.

Is Rebellion an inevitable part of the Muslim Teen's Life?

The way we answer the question of whether or not rebellion is an inevitable part of the life of a Muslim teen all depends on the way we define rebellion. If we define rebellion as the assertion of any sort of independence on the teen's part, then the answer to this question will no doubt be yes. But if we define rebellion more comprehensively, then we get a different, and might I say, more favourable answer.

Before tackling this issue, I think it's important to note that we, as Muslim parents, should not be opposed to our children being independent. Seeking independence is a normal trend and is perfectly natural for this stage of human development. By instilling in teens the desire for independence, Allah SWT is preparing them for the next stage of their life. They are undergoing a transition between childhood and adulthood. As such parents should not oppose it. Nor should parents resent the ability of their children to integrate well into their society, whether it be a majority Muslim society or a majority non-Muslim society. What we should be opposed to is our children following the norms and customs of their society blindly, and without regard for or reference to the teachings of the Quran and Sunnah. This would be a tragedy indeed. This would be called full assimilation, not integration. Our role as parents is to help our children intelligently integrate into their society. As Muslims we know that "Wisdom and good practices are the goal of a believer, wherever s/he find them s/he is the most deserving of using them." So if our children can learn to combine the best of both worlds as they say, by adopting the good of a culture and rejecting the bad, and of course, always abiding by the teachings of the Quran and Sunnah, then we will have done our job as parents.

When Muslim Teens Rebel: Causes and Solutions

If we define rebellion as resistance or defiance of any authority, control or tradition, then we also must decide what we are holding up as the authority, control or tradition that should be followed. And what more beautiful and worthy authority could one have than Allah (SWT) with His guidance, His mercy and His justice for all of mankind. This leads to another important note. Namely, that we as Muslim parents should be clear about one thing: that our loyalty lies with the Quran and Sunnah, not with the traditions and customs of our ancestors or our cultures back home. For it is the religion of Islam that was revealed to span all times and places, not my traditional Egyptian customs, or your conventional Pakistani traditions. The Qur'an strongly condemns those who blindly practice certain traditions and adhere to certain cultural norms, only based on what their ancestors used to practice without checking the validity of these practices in the environment or making sure that they don't contradict the orders of Allah SWT.[3]

Half the time, parents set themselves up for failure (and set their children up for almost guaranteed rebellion) by imposing way too many different types of authorities, controls and traditions in their children's lives. Not only is the child expected to follow the religious Islamic teachings, but they are also expected to conform to their parent's traditions from back home as well as their parents' personal preferences that may have absolutely no basis in the teachings of Islam. For example, some parents are completely opposed to their children watching any Hollywood movies, but pop in the latest Bollywood flick and the living room becomes the new site of a family reunion. What should matter here is not where a film was made, but the message the film conveys and whether or not it conforms to Islamic values. Parents should judge these things on a case by case basis and not assume that whatever comes from "that part of the world" is automatically evil and whatever comes from

---

3. (Q43, V22-23)

Is Rebellion an inevitable part of Muslim Teen's Life?

"our part of the world" is automatically good. We have to realize that by deciding to move our family to North America, or by remaining in the West and raising our children here, we are implicitly accepting the fact that they will be raised in a different culture and consequently, have a different cultural reference point. However, this does not mean that they have to lose their religion too. For that is the beauty of the true religion of Islam, it is flexible and pervasive enough to apply everywhere, at anytime. It does not grow old, out-dated, old-fashioned or obsolete. On the contrary, it grows stronger and more precious as we come to see that it can be applied in every era to everyone.

That was the long answer to the question. And now for the short answer. Is rebellion an inevitable part of the Muslim teen's life? It doesn't have to be, let's find out how…

Causes of Teen Rebellion

INTRODUCTION

In this chapter, we will try to cover the causes of teen rebellion. We will discuss the general causes of teen rebellion, such as the nature of the adolescent stage, peer pressure, cultural and generational gaps, TV, movies, video games, and play station culture. We will also take a look at Muslim teens and see if there are other factors contributing to them being rebellious. This is important because Muslim teens are in a unique situation and if we have to try to propose a solution to their problem, we have to understand the underlying causes of their problem for the solution to be effective.

TEENS IN GENERAL

Among the main causes of teen rebellion is the nature of the adolescent stage, peer pressure, the generation gap between parents and teens, and the current TV, movie, and video game culture.

THE NATURE OF THE ADOLESCENT STAGE: Teens during this stage are undergoing rapid and intense physiological and psychological changes. They want to be independent, but do not have the backlog of personal experience to function independently in the society to which they belong. They need to express personal needs and opinions and have them taken seriously. Also, they have not yet formed a cohesive value system that would support them in what to "live for," so this tremendously important anchor of security is not yet within reach. Although they are yearning for independence, they are still locked into financial and emotional dependence on their families. Another very important criterion of this stage is that teens vividly notice when there is a discrepancy between the rules and values espoused by adults and adult behavior. They also have

4

a strong need for adult mentoring and guidance and when the family unit fails to provide an environment that is nurturing and supportive, they turn to peers or celebrities for the fulfillment of these needs. They are in a transition stage moving from childhood to adulthood. The change of hormone levels in their bodies makes them experience quick mood swings and a very high level of sensitivity.

To elaborate more on the identity search, let us borrow the following few paragraphs from our book Muslim Teens: Today's Worry, Tomorrow's Hope: "If we could summarize the main issue teenagers are trying to deal with, it would be their search for an identity. The teen notices the changes that are taking place in his body. He realizes that he doesn't even have any control over them and he feels awkward. His body is undergoing a drastic process that he can't seem to keep up with. Certain questions start going through his mind. He wonders about what's happening to him and who he really is.

Soon, he also notices that his friends and classmates are changing and beginning to look different. Some of them are even acting different. He asks himself, "Where do I fit in to all of this? What's my place? Who are my real friends and do they still like me?"

More than anything, a teen wants to be part of the group; he wants to be liked by those around him; he wants to fit in, even if that means copying those around him." [4]

All of the above changes represent great challenges for the teen and contribute to them having a tendency to rebel against certain orders and instructions particularly from their parents.

PEER PRESSURE: This is a reality in the life of all teens, particularly during their high school years. The need to belong and fit in with their peer group is genuine and constitutes tremendous pressure on teens. Because the teen is so driven by the need to fit into a peer group, she

4. Drs. Ekram & Mohamed R. Beshir *"Muslim Teens, Today's Worry, Tomorrow's Hope;*   *A Practical Islamic Guide,"* amana publications, Beltsville, MD. 2003

might want to dress like her friends and follow the fashion trends. There is also a yearning to be part of the popular group at school: to look, talk, and act like them; to use the kind of language they use, even if it's inappropriate or rude; to watch the same movies and TV shows they watch; to listen to the same music they listen to; to go to their "hang-outs", and so on.

Feeling rejection from his peer group is such a painful thought for the teen that he is willing to do anything to avoid it. He strongly feels that anything he does to be part of the crowd is well worth the sacrifice

Considering all the negative aspects of popular teen culture in North America, such as promoting individuality, enjoyment and fun, physical indulgence and following fashions, short term thinking as well as challenging authority, it is easy to understand that such peer pressure would lead to rebellion on the part of teens

• GENERATION AND CULTURE GAP: Teens and their parents live in different times, and so, despite living in the same house and being part of the same family, they have different points of reference for such basic things as their values and their etiquettes. Lack of good parenting skills and effective communication, as well as lack of knowledge of the teen's environment on the parent's part, contributes negatively and widens the gap even further between parents and their teens. This puts significant stress on the relationship between teens and their parents.

• CURRENT TV, MOVIE, AND VIDEO GAME CULTURE: The amount of violence in TV programs, movies, and video games is increasing at an exponential rate. In her insightful book, Mayhem, a study of the impact of violence in the media on society, Dr. Sissela Bok, quotes a frightening statistic from research done in the early 1990s that estimated that "by the time a child left elementary school he or she would have watched 8,000 murders and more than 100,000 acts of violence on television, in the movies and video games."[5] In addition to the above, the very apparent disrespect for parents and elders (old folks), portrayed in most TV programs as well as the negative image about authority figures in general (Parents, Teachers, etc.) is a main contributor to the ill behaved response and "I don't care" attitude adopted by teens towards elders in general. Moreover, research also indicates that current video games can make players aggressive and insensitive to other people's needs as well as it triggers the same violent responses in the brain as actual aggression. This culture, no doubt, contributes to teen rebellion because it normalizes violence and promotes aggressive and antisocial behaviour.[6]

MUSLIM TEENS IN PARTICULAR

In addition to the above causes of rebellion for teens in general, there are additional causes for Muslim teens in particular that contribute to them being rebellious. Some of these are being part of a visible minority, being torn between two cultures, the need to belong, pressures on Muslim families, and lack of parenting skills and knowledge on the parents' part.

BEING PART OF A VISIBLE MINORITY: Some Muslim teens, because they wear the hijab or because they are people of colour, are a visible minority. This, of course, makes them stand out from their peers and adds to the pressures they face. You can imagine how difficult this is in high school, where wearing a different brand of jeans or shopping at a different store than your peers can cause them to mercilessly make fun of you, let alone wearing a hijab.

TORN BETWEEN TWO CULTURES

POPULAR TEEN CULTURE: As mentioned above, teen pop culture promotes challenging authority and individuality to the point of selfishness.

---

5. Dr. Sissela Bok; "Mayhem, a study of the impact of violence in media on society"

6. For more information on violence in TV refer to chapter 3 of our book *"Meeting the Challenge of Parenting in the West, An Islamic Perspective"* amana publications, third edition 2003

It also promotes indulging in constant fun without regard for responsibilities or consequences, always glorifying short-term thrills. Also, spiritual nourishment and soul elevation is not at all part of this culture. Following fashions is another very important norm of popular teen culture. Every season there is a new fashion and those who are not following these new styles and changing so they can conform with the new fashions are not "in". They are looked at rather strangely and are considered backward.

ISLAMIC VALUES: Islamic values promote the exact opposite, teaching believers to think of justice and responsibilities over fun and games. The rights of the individual are in balance with the rights of the community at large in Islamic law. Islamic values also promote thinking ahead to the consequences before undertaking any actions, not just ahead in this life, but also in the hereafter. Respect is a very important characteristic in Islam and the majority of Muslims try to raise their children to exercise respect in all their relationships (with parents, teachers, elders in the community, figures of authority, etc.) Also Islamic teachings highly regard the characteristic of *Haya'* (modesty, decency, bashfulness, and a rightly balanced amount of shyness) to the extent that Prophet Muhammad SAAW considered it as the main characteristic of Islam.[7] *Haya'* is also considered a branch of faith.[8] Popular teen culture doesn't promote *haya'* at all. As a matter of fact, if it promotes something, it is promoting non *haya'*.

It is apparent that the two cultures completely contradict each other, and so Muslim teens find themselves caught between two clashing worlds, living in one during the day and another by night.

Making matters even worse, some parents throw their country of origin's culture into the mix, insisting that their children practice certain

---

7. In the collection of *ahadeeth* of Albukhary, it was reported that prophet Muhammad SAAW said; There is a main character for every religion, and the main Character of Islam is *Haya'*

8. It was reported in the collection of *ahadeeth* of Albukhary that prophet Muhammad SAAW said; Faith is over seventy branshes, the highest of it is to witness that there is no deity but Allah and the lowest is to remove harmful matters from the road and *Haya'* is a branch of faith

cultural norms that have nothing to do with faith or Islam. This further overwhelms the teens who are already grappling with enough differences between themselves and their peers and can't understand why they have to worry about "how it's done" in Pakistan or Egypt, when they live here in North America.

NEED TO BELONG AND NEED FOR APPROVAL: The need to belong is one of the basic needs for every human. Everyone likes to feel that s/he is part of a bigger group or a bigger entity. Humans only feel that they are part of the bigger group when they share common activities with the group. Developmental psychology has found that children go through mainly two stages as far as their need for approval is concerned. The first stage starts from a very young age until approximately the pre-teen years (8-10 years old). At this stage, children are mainly seeking approval from their parents. They want their parents to be happy with them and to approve of their actions and behaviour. But this stage doesn't continue forever. A change starts taking place and slowly, children start noticing what's going on around them with other children and want to be like them. By the time they reach the adolescent stage, it is normal and expected for teens to seek the approval of their peers. This is more important to them than their parents' approval. This means that they want to fit in with their friends and at school, and being different causes them great stress and could be a leading reason for them to rebel against some of their parent's instructions, particularly when these instruction could make them stand out and not conform with pop teen culture.

PRESSURES ON MUSLIM FAMILIES: Many Muslim families are made up of immigrant parents who face immense challenges in their new environments. New to a country, they may have to learn and adapt to the norms of a new culture and language. Often, they must work long hours, studying for equivalency exams and renewing qualifications in order to obtain licenses to practice their professions in their new countries, while at the same time working low-paying jobs that they are overqualified for in order to support themselves and their families. Furthermore, most of them must do all of this without the support (financial, practical, or emotional) of any extended family.

Even Muslim families that are not immigrants face challenges living in a majority non-Mulsim society due to the differences in our value system. As a community, we lack many of the support systems and institutions that help families when they hit a rough patch. It is hard, if not impossible, in most cities to find a qualified Muslim counselor who can help families by providing such services as marriage counseling or family counseling. In many communities there is also a lack of Islamically acceptable social activities. This puts an added pressure on parents who always have to plan and organize for any community social activity, rarely being able to relax and socialize themselves.

The generation and cultural gap is also more severe between Muslim parents and their children. A good number of Muslim parents (particularly immigrant mothers) may not master the English language. This contributes negatively to their knowledge of their teen's environment and consequently it widens the gap further. One of the side effects of this, in some cases, is that teens look down at their parents because they lack the language skills and knowledge of their environment.

LACK OF KNOWLEDGE OF ISLAMIC PARENTING SKILLS ON THE PARENTS' PART: When parents lack knowledge and parenting skills they tend to fall back on old habits, using the ways that their parents used with them. These methods, being from a different time and, sometimes, a different place, are often irrelevant and ineffective. The words of wisdom we started the book with by Ali Ibn Aby Taleb RAA prove very valuable to parents in such situations. However, many of them don't pay much attention to this, even when it is pointed out to them by a friend or a scholar. They find it easier to continue using the same methods, even if they don't bear any useful fruits, rather than accept the fact that they have to change the way they deal with their children. Not only this, but they also tend to justify their behaviour by blaming the children, and blaming everything else but themselves. It looks like because change requires effort and hard work on their part, some parents are reluctant to accept that the responsibility is theirs because it means starting the process of change.

Here is a real life experience to illustrate this dilemma:

"In a recent convention that I participated in, the organizers wanted to get the ball of communication rolling between parents and their teens. As such, they had a session on bridging cultural and generational gaps. The session was divided into two parts. The first part was with parents and teens separately. In separate rooms, a couple of speakers talked with the parents, and another couple of speakers talked with the youth. I was among the speakers who talked with the parents. The idea was to get the parents to recognize that there is a real gap between them and their teens, which many of them refused to accept; moreover, they simply blamed the problem on teens not obeying their parents when being instructed to do something, which is a very superficial assessment of the issue. In an effort to make them realize the gravity of the situation, the speakers posed several questions to the parents and asked them to think about them. At this point, some of them agreed that there is a real gap and that they have to do something about it. The speakers solicited the parents' input in the form of concerns that could be presented in the second part of the session to both parents and youth to see how the youth feel about them. They would also be given a chance to discuss how they can start improving the communication between parents and their teens in an effort to bridge this gap. Although it was a very difficult exercise because of the reluctance of parents to accept any shortcomings on their part, we were able to come up with a list of concerns and fears for the second part of the session.

The speakers who worked separately with the youth had a much easier time. There was no need for them to go over many things to prove that there is a cultural and generational gap between them and their parents. They all agreed that the gap exists and started working on the nature of the relationship between them and their parents and how it could improve.

In the evening, the second part of the session, where both parents and youth were available, took place. The speakers who worked with the parents presented the parents' concerns and fears to the audience and those who worked with the youth did the same. Interestingly enough, the youth had chosen to draw pictures describing their relationships with their parents. As they say, "A picture speaks a thousand words." These drawings were hung on the walls around the room. They were very expressive and said a lot about how those young people viewed their relationship with their parents. Very few of the pictures reflected positive messages such as parental love and care. But the majority of pictures reflected a relationship that is dominated by parents and full of orders and demands placed on the youth, doesn't include respect to the teens in any way, shape or form, and in many cases was also full of violence as a disciplining mechanism. One drawing in particular listed all kinds of objects that parents used to hit and discipline the child with such as sticks, frying pans, hands and feet, etc. Surprisingly enough, the same drawing included a big heart. When the youth group who produced this drawing was asked about it, they said that, after hitting them, their parents would say that they are doing this because they love them.

From the teens' drawings, it was very clear that a great number of parents are using force as a method of discipline to correct the behaviour of their children. Realizing this, I felt it was my duty to state Islam's position on this issue. I indicated to the audience that force is not recommended in Islam and Prophet Muhammad SAAW never hit a child or a lady.[9] I also pointed out that there are many other good ways to discipline our children before resorting to using force. Force only suppresses behaviour, but proper disciplining, as advised by the Prophet Muhammad SAAW, changes behaviour for the better.

After the convention, I received an e-mail from a frustrated mother who accused me of taking the side of the youth during the entire session and not supporting the parents enough. This email goes to further show that parents are resisting change (even if it's for the better) and acting like ostriches who bury their heads in the sand and don't want to see the problem for what it is, thinking it will go away if we-the speakers- just continue to reprimand the youth/teens and tell them to respect their parents and obey them. We always emphasize respect for parents, particularly during sessions that are for teens only. However, we feel we also have to point out to parents their mistakes and correct their perspective on this very important issue. Parents have a great role to play and should be courageous enough to accept responsibility and start the process of change in their own ways of doing things, to adopt proper parenting techniques and change their habits for the sake of their children

Again, the lack of Islamic parenting techniques on the parent's part creates an unhealthy family atmosphere full of tension between parents and children. Such an atmosphere breads conflicts and confrontations between parents and teens, negatively contributes to widening the gap between them and may lead to defiance and rebellion on the teen's part.

---

9. For a detailed discussion on this issue supported by evidence from the teachings of Prophet Muhammad SAAW, please refer to our book *"Answers to Frequently Asked Questions on Parenting."* Part 1. amana publications, 2005.

Signs of Rebellion

There are various signs of rebellion that parents should be on the lookout for, some more serious than others. If you notice your child doing some or all of the following things, it is a good indication that your child is trying to rebel and disconnect him or herself from the Muslim identity. Of course, some teens may exhibit some of the following behaviours within moderation and still be proud of their Islamic identity. But generally, the following behaviours by teens should serve as a red flag that something is wrong.

When teens change their names or choose nicknames that disguise their Muslim identity. So if Ahmed starts asking people to call him Ed and Samir starts going by Sam, this could be a sign of more to come.

When teens insist on wearing what is "in", no matter how it conflicts with Islamic rulings of how to dress.

This applies to both girls and boys, though it may be more obvious with girls. Even if your daughter is not ready to don the hijab, modesty should still prevail and she should still know that there are limits. This means that she should still be encouraged to wear clothing that is not revealing or tight so that she can gradually work her way to wearing the hijab sometime in the future insha Allah.

Things to watch for with boys: the messages on their T-shirts, the shorts they wear, how much time they spend gelling their hair, wanting to dye their hair, or pierce their ears or wear gold jewellery etc. These days, the t-shirt industry is booming with the production of basic t-shirts that display certain images or messages on them. Some of these t-shirts are funny, others are downright wrong. Unfortunately, the ones selling the fastest are those that display rude or inappropriate messages, often containing swear words and references to sexuality. By wearing these types of clothing, one is ultimately promoting these types of values and our children should be taught to use their common sense and Islamic values to judge which messages are appropriate and which are inappropriate to parade around on our clothing. Our young men also need to be aware of the Islamic hijab for men. This means that short shorts and skin-tight pants, even if they are the current trend, are not suitable. In general then, parents should keep an eye out for how far their kids are willing to go to fit into the popular teen culture. Fitting in is not always a bad thing, and children need to feel that they belong at least in some ways to the society they live in, but if your teens are sacrificing important Islamic values and beliefs to melt right in with their friends then this is a sign of rebellion.

Listening to music with bad messages. Popular teen culture is regularly flooded with music from pop bands and solo singers all trying to make a buck from a naïve audience who will often soak up catchy tunes like sponges. Some bands sing about love, love and more love, while others sing about partying, death, drugs, hopelessness and suicide. Whatever the case may be, it is important to be aware of the message a song is transmitting as well as how it is transmitting that message. For example, even if a song seems to have a good meaning (ie it is against war and violence) if the singer decides to sing about his hate for war by screaming and swearing every second word, then your teen should not be listening to that song. Likewise, if a singer uses beautiful prose to sing about and describe the love of his life, that too is inappropriate. Thus it is important to be aware of not only the message a song is sending but also the way it is sending it.

When teens use bad or disrespectful language and take on the "bad boy" image. The language your teens use and the personas they take on can tell you a lot about where they may be headed. For example, if you notice that your teenage son has suddenly developed a limp in his walk that is not due to a medical reason, something could be up. If he starts to insert the words "dog" and "ayight" randomly in his speech, maintains a perfectly dirty room and addresses people in a disrespectful way then chances are he's going for the "bad boy" image that is usually a sign of rebellion.

When Teens lie about their activities. If you catch your son or daughter lying about where they were, what they were doing or who they were with, this is not a good sign. Chances are, they are hesitant to tell you the truth for a reason, probably because they don't think you will approve of the truth.

Other major signs of rebellion. Some other, more serious signs of rebellion include, skipping school, getting suspended from school, staying out past their curfew, smoking, drinking, and doing drugs. If you suspect that your teen is doing any of these things, it is very important that you help him or her right away. In some cases, such as the case of a child getting suspended from school, it is important to sit down with him/her and hear his/her full account of what happened. The problem may be deeper than it appears (such as harassment at school etc.) and only by listening to the teen can we uncover the real reason for this behaviour.

Why is it important to know and recognize these signs of rebellion in our youth? So that we can address the issue before it's too late. For example, if you notice that your son Anas Ud Deen is being referred to as ADD by all his friends, than you can try to jump in and help him before he starts rebelling in other, more drastic ways. You can try to get Anas involved in more Muslim youth activities, and you can make yourself available for Anas more often, in order to spend quality time together and give him a chance to open up to you about anything that he may be dealing with in his life that he would like to talk about. You can also try to ensure that Anas is spending his free time with people who will have a positive influence on him and won't drag him down into the dismal realm of partying, drinking and drugs.

Solutions

INTRODUCTION

The solution to teen rebellion is not a simple one since the problem itself is complicated and has many sources contributing to it. The solution has to be a multifaceted solution to take care of the various causes. It should be composed of three main components: benefiting from the Prophet's example in dealing with youth, parents taking on their responsibility, and the participation of the community. Let us now elaborate on these components.

PROPHETIC EXAMPLES WITH YOUTH

There are many great examples in the teachings of Prophet Muhammad SAAW related to dealing with teenagers and youth. All these examples and incidents can provide parents with wonderful guidelines on how to interact with youth. To try to enumerate these teachings would need a whole book by itself. As such, in this section we will refer to only a few incidents, the first of which is a very vivid one which will provide us with the most important guidance in this regard.

THE YOUTH WHO ASKED PERMISSION TO FORNICATE

This incident was reported in the collection of *Hadeeth of Imam Ahmad*. It is as follows:

"It was reported that a young man came to the prophet SAAW asking for permission to fornicate. Those around the prophet shouted at the young man. The prophet SAAW said, 'Bring him closer to me.'

He then asked him, 'Would you like it for your mother?'
The man said, 'No.'
The prophet SAAW asked him, 'Would you like it for your sister?'

17

The man replied, 'No.'

The prophet SAAW asked him, 'Would you like it for your aunt?'

He replied, 'No.'

The prophet SAAW asked him, 'Would you like it for your cousin?'

The man said, 'No.'

Then, the prophet SAAW told him, 'Likewise, other people would also not like it for their female relatives.' And he put his hand on the young man's chest and prayed saying: O Allah forgive his sin, purify his heart, and grant him chastity."[10]

LESSONS LEARNED

There are several lessons we can learn from this great dialogue between the prophet SAAW and this young man. Here are some of them:

• **Stay focused, control your emotions, and deal with the issue in a comprehensive way while staying calm.** Controlling our emotions and being calm while we are discussing issues with our youth is key to the success of the discussion. If a person is angry and emotional, it will put the teen on the defensive and s/he may not open up or even hear what the other person is saying. As such, it is important to train ourselves to be calm, not agitated, and focused. It is also important to get to the bottom of the issue and think about a comprehensive solution rather than just shouting and yelling at the young person and telling him/her as some parents do: "how dare you think about such a thing?!!! Don't you know that this is haram. You are a Muslim and Muslims don't do such things."

• **Closeness during discussion:** The Prophet SAAW asked the young man to get nearer and to sit very close to him. This is an indication that he is concerned about this young man and his affairs. It is an indication that he values him; he is interested in helping him to get over his weak-

---

10. Collection of *hadeeth* of Imam Ahmad

ness and find a solution for his case. Such action brought comfort to this young man and made him feel that the Prophet SAAW is making a genuine effort to listen to his case with an open mind and provide him with the best advice. It is important to understand this point and as parents we should try our best to practice it. Rather than shouting at the young person from afar, it is better to ask him/her to come closer to us and discuss the issue with him/her in a very calm and objective way.

• **Use of dialogue**: This is a very important lesson for all of us. The Prophet SAAW didn't lecture the young man or instruct him directly with what he should do and shouldn't do. Instead, he engaged him in a very constructive dialogue. He engaged him in a dialogue that made sense to this young man and made him feel that he owns the problem and he has to work on the solution. The use of dialogue in discussion is a very effective way of getting the message across and making the person feel that he contributed positively to the final solution. It also takes away the feeling of guilt that a person may have, particularly when a large group of people are around and witnessing the discussion.

• **Reasoning and explaining**: Our faith is logical and all the orders of Allah SWT are for our own benefit. As such, there is a logical explanation and reason for every prohibition in our *Deen* and for every permitted and allowed act. Muslim Scholars explained these reasons for us in a clear way. It is important for all Muslim parents to learn and understand these reasons clearly. This will help them to support their arguments when they dialogue with their teens and try to convince them to do or not do certain things. Teens and youth like to understand the reasons behind instructions. It is not enough to tell them to do something because they are Muslims. That doesn't help. They are faced with many questions from their peers and need answers that make sense and that they can use when they discuss with peers at school or friends in their neighborhood. The Prophet SAAW didn't just instruct this young man and tell him that fornication is prohibited. He reasoned with the young man to help the young man himself see the benefits of abstaining from such an act.

• **Use of examples that the teen can understand and relate to:** Using examples makes the message a person is trying to communicate very clear. The Prophet SAAW used examples often when giving advice to his companions to clarify certain issues to them and make them simple to understand. He described prayer by saying, "can you imagine that there is a river in front of your home that you use to wash yourself five times a day. Would it leave any dirt on you?" The companions said, "no it wouldn't." The Prophet SAAW said, "this is the example of the five daily prayers. Allah erases your mistakes with them." [11] In the incident we previously described, the Prophet SAAW used examples that the young man could relate to easily. He mentioned the young man's female relatives in a very clear way to drive the message across. With this it became very clear to this young man that this act is an awful act and no one should do it. Parents should learn from this wonderful lesson how to effectively communicate with their teens and young men.

• **Touch the heart and soul:** There is no doubt that the way Prophet Muhammad SAAW dialogued with this young man touched his heart and soul. He was very close to him. His words were soft and gentle. He didn't yell or shout at him. He touched his chest and made a wonderful dua' for him. He comforted him and continued to dialogue with him until he was convinced that he shouldn't commit such an act. The mercy and gentleness were pouring from his mouth in a very eloquent and convincing dialogue that would touch anyone's heart and soul. There is no doubt that this is another beautiful lesson for parents to follow.

• **Gentleness and expressing genuine care:** It is reported by Aishah RAA that the messenger of Allah SAAW said, "Allah is gentle and loves gentleness

---

11. Agreed Upon

in every thing."[12] Aishah RAA also reported that Prophet Muhammad SAAW said, "Allah is gentle and He rewards abundantly for practicing gentleness more than anything else."[13] She RAA also reported that Prophet Muhammad SAAW said, "gentleness and kindness adorn everything and if they are withdrawn from anything that makes it defective and ugly."[14] The Prophet SAAW practiced this gentleness with this young man at the highest level. The man felt that Muhammad SAAW genuinely cared for him. To the prophet SAAW, this young man was a real person and one from the Muslim Ummah that he cared for so much, to the extent that Allah SWT described him in the Qur'an as "very keen about the believers affairs, kind and merciful towards them."[15] The Prophet SAAW's expressing such genuine care and mercy no doubt had a positive impact on this young man's feelings and helped greatly in comforting him and taking these bad thoughts completely out of his mind. Parents can nourish their relationship with their teens and youth and strengthen their bonds with them with a sprinkle of gentleness and a touch of genuine care.

• **Use of *Dua'*:** *Du'a* is a very powerful tool that is frequently neglected by Muslims in spite of many instructions in the Qur'an and the teachings of Prophet Muhammad SAAW to make *dua'*. As a matter of fact, he taught us a *dua'* for almost every occasion. It is our duty to learn these *dua's* and use them whenever we need Allah's help, which is so often. We also should beg of Allah regularly to help us do the right thing and raise our children to have strong and confident Muslim personalities. Of course, we have to do our share in terms of learning and practicing the proper Islamic parenting principles and skills as well as exerting the effort to do things right. The use of *dua'* should not be undermined nor should doing our share be neglected. A combination of both will, insha'a Allah, bring the required results as they did with this young man.

---

12. Agreed Upon
13. Muslim
14. Muslim
15. Q 9, V 128)

• **Not giving in to the culture's social norms**: This specific lesson needs a bit of elaboration. It is a very important lesson for all parents. A great majority of parents respond to events in their children's lives spontaneously without thinking. They repeat certain patterns that they learned from their own experiences or their cultural backgrounds. It is important to note here that not all cultural practices we use are Islamic and good, even if they are practiced in the majority of Muslim countries. Some of the cultural practices are derived from teachings of the Prophet SAAW as well as Islamic values, but others are not. It is our duty, as Muslims living here in North America, not to blindly follow our ethnic practices without ensuring that they don't contradict Islamic values.

It is clear from this incident that the companions were practicing the social norm of the time. They tried to push this young man around, shouted and yelled at him as soon as he asked such a question. The Prophet Muhammad SAAW didn't cave in to such social norms. He instructed the companions RAA not to do this, asked them to bring the young man closer to him and used the opportunity to teach them the proper way of dealing with such issues. We know that deviating from cultural practices may not be the easiest thing to do at certain times particularly when others are sticking to such practices. We also appreciate the heaviness of being different and the burden it brings with it. However, the cause is so noble and the reward is magnificent and nice that it is worth it to make the effort and change our ways of doing things. You will be rewarded in three ways for doing this. First, you will be rewarded for obeying Allah's order to follow Prophet Muhammad SAAW. Secondly, you will be rewarded for following the way of Prophet Muhammad SAAW, which will bring Allah's love to you. Thirdly, you will be rewarded for the effort you make to bring somebody closer to Allah and make him/her love and live by His *deen*. So next time insha'a Allah you find yourself falling back to certain cultural practices that may not be helpful in improving the relationship between you and your teen, and strengthening your bond with them, remember not to give in to these practices and to follow your role model, Prophet Muhammad SAAW, and his Prophetic guidance.

Another very important point to note in this *hadeeth* is that the young man was asking the Prophet SAAW to do something that is completely not permitted (very clearly *haram*), yet he SAAW discussed with him and took the time to explain and dialogue in a way that convinced the young man not to ask about this again. Compare this with the reaction of some parents when their child asks them to do something that is not necessarily *haram* in itself, but may not be to the liking of the father or the mother. The answer is an emphatic no without any discussion. Some of them may say: "I said NO, end of discussion," without giving the child any chance to ask why and without even giving an explanation as to why s/he is not supposed to do such things.

Next time your teens request to go to the movies with their friends, please take some time and ask them a few questions. Direct them to find out what the movie is about and if there are any objectionable scenes or language in the movie. Allow them to do some research and find these things out rather than saying no upfront without discussing the matter. This way they will know why they are not allowed to watch such material. If the research shows that the movie is clean, there's no problem in allowing them to go.

Next time your teen asks you that s/he wants to visit a non-Muslim friend or schoolmate don't say no upfront. Don't cut the discussion short without asking questions in order to find out more about the friend and his/her family. Even try to visit their home and get to know the parents of this friend first hand. If they are people of value and their house is safe, there is nothing wrong with allowing your teen to spend some time visiting with them. Having friends is a natural need for our teens and as parents we should try our best to acknowledge this need, help in fulfilling it, and teach our children how to select good friends rather than ignoring the need and closing the discussion with an emphatic no. This is your opportunity to teach your teen the wonderful advice of Prophet Muhammad SAAW in this regard, and how he warned us about the strong influence our friends have on us. It was reported by Abu Hurairah RAA that Prophet Muhammad SAAW said, "a man follows the religion of his closest friend, so each one should consider whom he makes his friend."[16] In another narration, Abu Musa al-Ash'ari RAA heard the Messenger of Allah SAAW saying, "good company and bad company are like the owner of musk and the iron smith. The owner of the musk will either offer you some musk free of charge, or you will buy it from him or smell its pleasant odour. As for the iron smith, either he will burn your clothes, or you will have to smell the repugnant smell of the iron."[17]

Next time your teen asks you to hang out at the mall after school for half an hour or so with his school friends, rather than saying no without discussion, use the chance to dialogue with him about time and the importance of utilizing our time properly. We emphasize here the word dialogue. Make sure it is done in a discussion form and not as a lecture or preaching. Remind him/her of some of the Qur'anic verses emphasizing the significance of time such as the many *Sura's* in chapter 30 of the Qur'an where Allah SWT makes an oath with time or part of time. Chat with him/her about how all *Ibadat* in Islam (*Salat, zakat,* fasting, and *Hajj*) are linked to time in one way or the other and how they contribute to helping Muslims value time and not wasting it. Make it an educational experience with your teen and you may allow him/her occasionally to hang out with their schoolmates, as long as it is not done excessively.

We're not promoting allowing our children to go to any movie, or to

16. Muslim
17. Agreed upon

be friends with anybody, or to waste their time hanging around in malls and shopping centers, but we're trying to make sure that parents speak, discuss, and dialogue with their teens before saying no. This is a great opportunity to teach your teen how to make informed decisions and not to be a follower.

Drinking after the Prophet SAAW

Another incident we can learn from is when the prophet SAAW was sitting with a group of his companions and he was given a container of milk to drink by the host. The tradition in such circumstances is to drink then pass the container to the person on the right to drink and so on. It happened that the person next to the Prophet SAAW on his right side was a young person (around 10 years old) and there were other older companions in the gathering. The Prophet SAAW didn't ignore this young man after he drank from the container. Rather, he asked him, "would you permit me to give the container to the older companion to drink first?" The young person said, "No, I would like to have the honor to drink after you." The Prophet SAAW gave him the container first to drink and then passed it around to the other companions. [18]

The above incident illustrates a very important lesson for all parents. The Prophet SAAW dealt with this young man in a very respectful way. He didn't ignore him and just give the container to the older companions. He took his permission first, and when the young person said that he wants to drink first, the Prophet SAAW respected his wish and didn't pressure him to change his mind. Respect is a very important quality in Islam and Muslims are supposed to respect everyone irrespective of their age, color, ethnic background, or gender.

Parents usually require their children to treat them with respect; however, they themselves may not show much respect to their kids. The above

---

18. Agreed Upon

example of the Prophet SAAW is a compelling and vivid illustration of the importance of respect in all relationships. Dealing with our children in a respectful way is a key for them to learn respect. After all, modeling is the most effective method of parenting. It is unrealistic to expect respect from our children when we ourselves are not showing them respect in the way we deal with them. The Prophet SAAW always modeled for his companions. He never asked them to do anything without him doing it first. He asked them to pray five daily prayers, but he did even more. In addition to the five obligatory prayers, he prayed many extra prayers. He also did the same with fasting and charity. This is a great lesson for all parents.

MAKING A PLEDGE WITH YOUTH

Here is another wonderful example from the life of Prophet Muhammad SAAW that we can learn from in the area of dealing with teens and youth: It was reported by Ali Ibn Aby Taleb RAA that when the qur'anic verse "And warn your close kinship"[19] was revealed, the Prophet SAAW gathered his close relatives and invited them to Islam indicating that he is a messenger from Allah SWT and he is ordered to convey the message to them in particular and to the rest of people in general. None of the older generation, such as his uncles or aunts followed him. The only person who accepted his invitation was Aly Ibn Aby Taleb RAA who was already a Muslim in private but had never made his Islam public until that day.[20] He was a young man in his teens. When Aly Ibn Aby Taleb RAA said, "I believe in you and I accept to follow you o' Prophet of Allah," the Prophet SAAW stretched his hand out to him and said, "Extend your hand so I can make a pledge with you."[21]

---

19. (Q26, V214)
20. *Muneer Al-Ghadban, "Al-Manhag Al-Haraky llseerah Al Nabaweiah"* 10th edition, page 34, 21. *Al-Wafa'* for printing, publishing and Distribution, *Al Mansourah*, Egypt, 1998 Imam Ahmad

This action of the prophet SAAW indicated that he was treating Aly Ibn Aby Taleb RAA, the young teen, as an adult. Such treatment would no doubt make him feel the seriousness of the matter and would elevate his self esteem and help in making him a strong and confident Muslim. This treatment also would contribute positively to the emotional development of Aly Ibn Aby Taleb RAA and make him a mature and responsible person who can carry out duties, fulfill commitments, and respect his agreements and covenants with others.

This is a great lesson for parents to help their children develop strong and confident personalities and who be proud of their identities as Muslims and can carry out duties and fulfill responsibilities. Trust your teens and take them seriously, and they will step up to the plate, carry the torch, face the challenge, and do their share successfully under your wise mentorship and guidance.

PARENTS' ROLE

The parents have to carry out a great portion of the solution to the teen rebellion problem. They have to work on various fronts: the first of these is to learn from the Prophet's example in dealing with youth and to try to implement it. Another front is to understand and learn Islamic parenting principles to use them in parenting their teens. For parents to succeed in following the Prophet's example, and putting the Islamic parenting principles they learn into practice, they have to continuously assess and evaluate the way they parent their children and modify it to get the best results.

SELF SEARCH AND SELF IMPROVEMENT

This is the process of holding oneself accountable for what he or she is doing and trying to correct one's actions to get the best results in any given area of life. This process is a central theme in Islam and is recommended by verses of Qur'an and sayings of Prophet Muhammad SAAW as well as practices of his companions.[22] This process consists of six steps. These are search, evaluate, acknowledge, reinforce, change, and hang on. Let us now elaborate on each step of these steps:

Search within ourselves and review all the actions and parental behaviours that we use with our children. We must dig deep into our past, thinking back to childhood, and uncover any hidden reasons that might be the source of our parental behaviour. Often, we may be talking to our children in a certain way, and if we stopped to think about it, we would realize that we are doing exactly what our mom or dad used to do with us.

Evaluate the actions and sayings we use in dealing with our children. Which of these actions are positive, supportive, and based on Islamic values and teachings, and which of these actions are negative, unsupportive, and have no basis in Islamic teachings? An example of a negative action is when we, as parents, try to resolve a conflict with our child while we are angry. If we yell, shout, and fight with the child just to vent our anger, we are using a negative parental behaviour. However, if we control our anger by using the anger management techniques prescribed to us by our beloved Prophet SAAW, teach our child to do the same, and then discuss the problem calmly, we are using a positive parental behavior.

Acknowledge our findings and categorize them as either positive or negative behaviours. Again, the positive ones are those that agree with Islamic teachings, are suitable for the environment, and help our children become strong and confident Muslims. The negative behaviours are those that are mainly from inherited tradition, have no basis in Islamic teachings, may not be suitable for the environment, and may make our

---

22. Consult with our book *"Parenting Skills according to Qur'an and Sunnah"* amana publications, Beltsville, MD, 2004 for further information on evidence of the process from Qur'an and teachings of Prophet Muhammad SAAW

children feel defeated as Muslims. Acknowledging our strengths and weaknesses is the first step in improving our parental behaviour. After that, we have to put our trust in Allah SWT and make a commitment to positive change. Changing unhealthy habits is the key to success, as the great scholar Ibn al-Qayyim said, "and the core of the matter is in leaving out the unhealthy, inherited habits."

Reinforce the positive parental behaviours and keep practicing them with our children. If they work, we must continue using them.

Change the negative parental behaviours and replace them with positive ones. We have to work hard at this because change does not come easily. It takes hard work to change habits, so we have to be patient and keep trying. Changing bad habits into good ones is worth the struggle. The expected benefits in our children's development are too important for us not to try our best to change these habits. When trying to change our bad habits or negative parenting behaviour, we should follow the advice of the Prophet SAAW and always perform *salat-ul-hajah*, the prayer of need, and make *du'a* intensively, to help us in the process of trying to become a better parent. In addition, we must repeat this prayer a few times, rather than just performing it once.

Hang On We cannot give up right away. We should put our trust in Allah and keep trying. As parents, we can learn new ways and improve on our old ways. The positive results will be certain if we follow the above steps. It may take longer than we think, but we can't give up. The reward will be tremendous if we work hard and make a sincere effort to become better parents. [23]

While doing this self search process, we consistently seek Allah's support through regular and intensive dua'a to help us achieve our goals.

---

23. For more information about the self-search process and practical examples of positive and negative parental behaviours, please see *"Parenting Skills According to Qur'an and Sunnah"* By Drs. Ekram & Mohamed Beshir, amana publications, Beltsville, MD, 2004

We also seek Allah's help to strengthen us by doing *Salatul-Hajah*.[24]

IMPORTANT ISLAMIC PARENTING PRINCIPLES

This is the second most important thing that parents have to do to help avoid teen rebellion. They should understand, learn, and practice Islamic Parenting methods and principles. In some of our previous books,[25] we collected over 40 of these principles. For each of them we stated the principle, quoted either a verse from the Qur'an or one of the Prophet's sayings, or an event from his *Seerah* as evidence to the principle, and we also provided the reader with two practical examples on how to use the principle with a young child and with an older child (i.e. teenager). These principles include the following:

- Linking the child to Allah
- Understanding your child and parenting with knowledge
- Understanding your child's environment
- Providing a healthy, pleasant, loving, and positive family atmosphere
- Expressing love, gentleness, and kindness
- Sharing feelings
- Practicing mutual respect
- Brevity in preaching
- Never resorting to force
- Being fair to all
- Bonding on a personal level with each child
- Teaching them that every soul is accountable for what it earns (consequences)

---

24. *Salatul- Hajah* is a prayer for a need. The Prophet SAAW recommended that if you need the help of Allah in any matter, you try your best and seek His help via performing two *Raka'h* of prayer to Allah and making a certain Dua'a asking Allah to help you with this specific matter

25. *"Meeting the Challeng of Parenting in the West, an Islamic perspective," "Muslim Teens, Today's worry, Tomorrow's Hope," Parenting Skills Based on Qur'an and Sunnah"*, All published by amana publications 1998, 2001, 2004 respectively.

Solutions

- Providing opportunity for self corrections (Good deeds wipe out bad ones)
- Emphasizing positive action
- Being wise and picking your fights. Dealing with wisdom is your best asset as a parent
- Using a step by step and gradual approach to change undesired behaviours
- Using effective communications and active listening
- Reasoning, dialoguing, and discussing
- Utilizing what is best in all your dealings with teens
- Helping your child to be capable and develop skills
- Facilitating their being part of a larger community
- Helping them to understand the logical reasons for what is going on around them
- Providing healthy and suitable alternatives
- Controlling anger
- Teaching cooperation
- Fulfilling promises
- Utilizing opportunities
- Illustrating consequences in a vivid way
- Fulfilling their spiritual needs, touching their soul and awakening their conscience
- Using examples from their environment that they can relate to
- Using the rule of the lesser of two evils (avoiding the greater harm by committing the lesser harm)
- Not forcing them to pick up where you left off
- Forgiving and forgetting
- Following up and being consistent
- Teaching *Haya'*
- Using a holistic approach

- Having realistic expectations
- Training for accountability, respectability
- Providing positive peer pressure, and
- Working toward a common point of reference
- Etc.

Our intention is not to repeat the explanations of the above principles and talk about them in detail again. Our focus in this book will mainly be on some of the key Islamic parenting principles and methods mentioned above, such as knowledge; wisdom; effective communication; teaching and training children for accountability, responsibility, and respectability; providing healthy and suitable alternatives; being consistent; and providing healthy, pleasant, loving and positive family atmosphere. We feel that understanding these principles will have a direct impact on the solution to teen rebellion, which is the question at hand. We refer the readers to the references quoted above if they are interested in further details about the other principles. Let us now talk in detail about these critical principles

KNOWLEDGE

We feel that knowledge is a must for parents in the following areas:
- Teens' developmental stages,
- Teens' environment,
- Teens' need for approval, and
- General Islamic knowledge

Let us start first with general Islamic knowledge. It is critically needed for parents to make sure they teach their children what is right and what is wrong, what is *halal* and what is *haram*, and the wisdom behind various prohibitions. It will also allow parents to answer their teen's questions in an intelligent way that would help them to make sense out of what is going around them. When parents lack proper Islamic knowledge, and they hope to achieve certain results by just saying to their teens, "don't do this because you are a Muslim" without logically engaging them in an intelligent discussion that can help them with their outer environment, it doesn't work. Muslim teens face a very hostile environment outside their homes, and they need the proper knowledge to answer their colleagues' questions in an intelligent way that makes sense to them, as well as to their colleagues and non-Muslim friends. Parents tend to force their ideas on their teens through instructing and lecturing, thinking that this is enough for them to be good practicing Muslims. This is far from the truth. Dialoguing, reasoning, and explaining will certainly help. Having Islamic knowledge will also allow parents to teach their children Islamic history and tell them about historical personalities who could be looked to as great role models, rather than music composers, singers, actors/actresses, and sports figures. It will also help parents to teach their children the biography of Prophet Mohammad SAAW (*Seerah*) in a way that makes them closer to him and makes them love him as their ultimate role model.

The second area of knowledge is the teens' developmental stages and changes that take place within teens bodies and minds during the adolescence stage. A great many books talked about this subject. We also hinted at it in the first chapter of this book as part of the causes for teen rebellion. Chapter 1 of our book "Muslim Teens: Today's Worry, Tomorrow's Hope" provides a comprehensive overview on this topic.[26] Drastic physical, emotional, social, intellectual and psychological changes constitute an integral part of this stage. These changes make teens moody and very sensitive to comments, particularly from their parents. The search for identity and eagerness to achieve independence is another very important characteristic of the adolescent stage. Parents' knowledge of such attributes helps tremendously in knowing how to appropriately deal

---

26. Drs Ekram and Mohamed Rida Beshir; *"Muslim Teens: Today's Worry, Tomorrow's Hope"* amana publications, Beltsville, Maryland, USA, 2nd edition, third printing, 2007

with teens and how to use the proper language and body gestures to avoid embarrassing their teens and avoid pushing them into using a rebellious attitude.

The third area of knowledge is the teens' environment. There is no doubt that environment has very considerable effects on the behaviour of humans. Prophet Muhammad SAAW emphasized this on numerous occasions.[27] Teens' environment in North America is very confusing and full of all kinds of pressures, particularly for those who want to adhere to good morals and follow sound value system. Popular teen culture promotes exactly the opposite of what we try to instill in our Muslim teens. While Muslim parents want their teens to care for family and promote strong bonds among family members, care for other members of the community, and pay attention to the well being of the whole society they are living in, pop culture promotes individuality. It is mainly about what the individual wants and feels like doing without considering the rights of others or the consequences of their actions on the rest of society. While Muslim parents would like to raise their teens to carry out duties and practice self control and self elevation, so that not everything the teen wants, he or she can do, North American pop culture emphasizes fulfilling desires, enjoyment and fun. Pop culture wants fun in everything to the extent that the greeting used among almost everyone for examples when they leave home is "Have Fun." Compare this to the advice of Prophet Muhammad SAAW, who taught us to say, "In the name of Allah. I put my trust in Allah. Oh Allah, I seek refuge in you not to misguide any body or to be misguided; not to humiliate anybody or to be humiliated; not to oppress anybody or to be oppressed; and not to mistreat anybody or to be mistreated."[28] This is a wonderful *du'a* to help

27. See chapter 3 of our book *"Meeting the Challenge of Parenting in the West: An Islamic Perspective"*, amana publications, Beltsville, Maryland, USA, Third edition, 2003
28. Ibn Majah, Termidhi, abu Dawoud

us go out with the right attitude to face the challenges ahead of us, a *du'a* that teaches us how to behave and interact with others. Life is not all just for fun and enjoyment. There are serious things that we have to attend to in our life. Popular teen culture emphasizes physical indulgence and following fashions to the extent that there is always a new fashion, not only for each year, but even for every season. Those who don't adopt these new fashions are not considered "in". Those who don't embrace new fashions are not part of the popular group and are not accepted by others. Contrast this with modesty and spiritual nourishment that Islamic teachings call for. These are two completely different sets of values. There is also popular teen culture's emphasis on short-term gains and immediate gratification. Teens are encouraged to do whatever they feel like doing in the spur of the moment, irrespective of the consequences of their actions. Islamic teachings call for long-term planning and considering the consequences of our actions not only on ourselves, but also on other members of the community we live in and on humanity as a whole, and not only the consequences in this life on earth, but also after our death. Popular teen culture doesn't put a lot of weight on respecting authority figures in the life of teens such as parents, teachers, and elder community members. As a matter of fact, it is even considered heroic to challenge such figures of authority in society. On the other hand, Islamic teachings promote respect for everyone and particularly those in authority such as our teachers, our Imams, our parents, our scholars, and elder community members. Popular teen culture promotes the use of vulgar language and indecency to the extent that those who use this kind of language are considered cool and those who don't are not welcomed as part of the "in" group. Islamic teachings place decency (*Haya'*) and the use of good words in a very high and lofty position. Prophet Muhammad SAAW said, "for every Deen, there is a core character, and the core Character of Islam is *Haya'*"[29]

---

29. Ibn Majah

When Muslim Teens Rebel: Causes and Solutions

When parents have such an in depth knowledge of all these differences between popular teen culture and the value system they are trying
to instill in their teens and to make them live by, they realize that their
teens don't have it easy. Muslim teens are - as they say- stuck between a
rock and a hard place. With this knowledge, parents are in a much better
situation to appreciate their teens' circumstances and provide them with
the proper help needed.

The Fourth Area of knowledge is that of **teens' need for approval**. In
general, children are always looking for approval. They do something
then they wait to see if it is approved by those around them or not. The
source of approval changes for different age groups. From birth up to
almost 8 or 9 years old, children are mainly seeking the approval of their
parents. The younger they are, the more they are attached to their parents
and the more they like to imitate and repeat whatever parents do or say.
The approval of parents is very important to young children. However,
this stage doesn't last forever. A shift starts taking place slowly and gradually in the source of approval for kids. When they reach the adolescent
stage, they are strongly drawn to fit in with their peer group and the
approval of their peers means a lot to them. They want to talk like them,
walk like them, dress like them, and go to movies and participate in the
type of activities that the rest of the main stream are involved in. This is
a natural trend. If parents don't invest properly in building a strong sense
of Muslim identity in their kids during the first stage where parents'
approval is very important to the children, those when they reach the
teens stage they will be more susceptible to the negative effects of the popular teen culture.

To avoid the undesired aspects of popular teen culture, parents should
wisely invest in the relationship with their children during their younger
age. They should strive to create a strong emotional bond and an open
channel of communication between themselves and their children. The

earlier parents start, the more successful they will be in achieving their goal and in helping their children not to succumb fully to the ills of popular teen culture.

WISDOM, A GREAT ASSET

Wisdom is a great asset. Parents need wisdom as well as knowledge. Knowledge in itself is not enough. Wisdom will help parents to apply their knowledge properly. Wisdom is the parents' best friend, particularly when they deal with teens. Wisdom is needed to handle each situation according to its own merits. Wisdom is needed to make sure they don't compare their children to each other. Children are not all the same and wisdom is needed to find out the key to each child's personality and the best way to deal with that personality. Wisdom is needed by parents to pick their fights and make sure they overlook minor mistakes by their teens to strengthen the bond between them and their children, rather than straining the relationship by being picky. Wisdom is also needed to know when to say "No" and when to say "Yes". Not only this, but it is also needed to know when to replace "No" with "Yes" whenever you can because too many "No's" may have a drastic effect on the relationship with your teen and on the way he/she views Islam. Wisdom is needed for parents to appreciate the different environment our teens are living in and the types of pressures they are facing in this environment. Wisdom is also needed to ensure that parents can see the bigger picture of every situation and try to always choose the lesser of the two evils, rather than being stubborn and causing more harm by straining their relationship with their teens and letting the situation slip out of their hands.

EFFECTIVE COMMUNICATION

Effective communication is another very important Islamic parenting principle. It includes, among other things, brevity in preaching, active listening, use of dialogue, anger management, and being approachable.

The teachings of Prophet Muhammad SAAW emphasize all of the above aspects of communication.

First, he never bored his companions with lengthy lectures. He usually used proper occasions to admonish them and teach them certain lessons.[30]

He was always very attentive to anyone speaking to him and never interrupted anybody during his/her speech. He was the best active listener. His communication style was the best because he forever implemented the Qur'anic rule of communication, "and say to my servant to say what is best."[31]

Most of the time he, SAAW would use dialogue as a means of communication to prove his point and convince the other person of his point of view. The above encounter with the young man who was asking him for permission to fornicate is a great example of the Prophet's use of dialogue as an effective method of communication.

Another effective tool of communication is **anger management**. The Prophet SAAW emphasized this in many ways. Following is some of his advice in this regard:

• On the authority of Abu Huraira RAA who narrated that a man asked the Messenger of Allah, SAAW, to give him advice. He SAAW said, "Don't be angry." The man repeated his question several times and the Prophet replied several times, "Don't be angry."[32]

• In another agreed upon hadeeth, the Prophet, SAAW, defined the strong man as the one who controls himself in a fit of rage, and not the

---

30. "It was reported on the authority of *Abi Wa'il Shaqiq bin Salama RAA* that he said: *Ibn Mas'ud, RAA* used to preach every Thursday. A man said to him: Abu Abdur-Rahman, we like your talk, and we like that you deliver us a lecture every day. He said: There is nothing to hinder me in preaching and giving you a lecture every day, but I fear to bore you. I follow the same method in preaching to you that the Messenger of Allah, SAAW, adopted in preaching to us out of fear of boring us." (Agreed upon)

31. (Q 17, V 53)

32. Bukhari

one who wrestles others.

• On the authority of Mu'ath bin Anas RAA who narrated that the Prophet SAAW said, "The one who swallows up anger will be called out by Allah, the Exalted, to the forefront of the creatures on Resurrection Day and will be allowed to choose any pure-eyed virgin he will like."[33]

Not only did the Prophet SAAW warn us about getting angry, but he also taught us the best anger management techniques as follows:

• Seek refuge with Allah from Satan: On the authority of Suliman bin Surd RAA, two people began to quarrel with each other in front of the prophet SAAW. The face of one of them turned red and the veins of his neck were swollen. The messenger of Allah said, "I know of a saying that if he were to utter it, his fit of rage would be relaxed and that wording is: I seek refuge with Allah from Satan, the accursed." So the companions went to the man and told him that the messenger of Allah SAAW said to say "I seek refuge with Allah from Satan, the outcast."[34]

• Change your position: It was narrated that the messenger of Allah SAAW said, "If one of you gets angry while he's standing let him sit down, and if he is still angry let him lie down."[35]

• Performing *wudu*': It was narrated that the prophet SAAW said, "anger is from Satan and Satan is created from fire, and fire is extinguished by water; so if one of you becomes angry let him perform *wudu*'."[36]

• Be silent: It was narrated that the prophet SAAW said, "If one of you gets angry let him be silent."[37]

Parents should make use of all these wonderful techniques to manage their anger when they are in conflict with their children. Parents should not be quick to react when they are upset with their kids, but should use

---

33. *Abu Dawoud* and *Al Termethi*
34. Agreed upon
35. Ahmad
36. Abu Dawoud
37. Ahmad

the above strategies instead. It may be difficult at first, and it does take training, but these techniques are very helpful and make it a lot easier to avoid unnecessary problems. Parents should also teach their children these anger management techniques, and train them to use them.

Being approachable is the last component we would like to emphasize under effective communication. Among the plethora of advice Prophet Muhammad SAAW provided us with, there is one particular piece of advice that we think is key to the success of the parent-child relationship. He said:

"Whoever has a young child, let him act like a child with him/her."[38]

This is what every parent has to do to have a successful relationship with his/her children. We have to be approachable fathers and approachable mothers. Our children should be able to approach us with anything they have on their minds at any time. Providing a positive, warm and encouraging family atmosphere is key for a strong, healthy relationship between parents and children, particularly during the taxing adolescent years. On the other hand, being judgmental, yelling, and shouting doesn't help in having a strong bond and seeming approachable to our children. Our children shouldn't hesitate to approach us with all their problems. We feel that being approachable would undoubtedly be of great help to parents in the formidable task of ensuring that their children will not only grow up to be strong, confident Muslim personalities who can resist the various negative effects of the main stream North American environment, but furthermore, have a positive influence on their surroundings and feel comfortable with themselves.

TEACHING AND TRAINING CHILDREN FOR ACCOUNTABILITY, RESPONSIBILITY, AND RESPECTABILITY

The above three components, accountability, responsibility, and

---

38. Al-Jame' Al-Sagheer

respectability are very important and highly regarded values in Islam. Numerous verses of the Qur'an and practices of the Prophet Muhammad SAAW emphasize the fact that these are core principles and teachings of our *Deen* and recommend that parents promote and instill such values in their children. Emphasizing accountability and responsibility, the Qur'an states: "Every soul will be held accountable and responsible for what it earns."[39] Furthermore, the wonderful saying of the Prophet Muhammad SAAW reiterates this point: "Every one of you is in charge (is a guardian) of certain responsibilities and he or she is responsible and will be asked how they discharged their responsibilities."[40] Emphasizing respect, the Prophet SAAW, has said: "He is not one of us who does not have mercy on our young ones and does not have respect for our elders."[41] Training and teaching our children to practice these amazing virtues will, no doubt, help refine their character and help them resist succumbing to the low confrontational behaviour of rebelling against their parents. When these wonderful qualities are an integral part of our children's personalities, they will resort to amicable ways to resolve any conflicts with their parents. They will behave in a respectable way and will value their relationship with their parents highly. They will be very careful not to damage this important relationship just to blend in with main stream teens and to appear to be following the popular teen culture.

Educating and training our children for accountability, responsibility, and respectability will definitely go a long way in helping them to avoid being rebellious.

It is of utmost importance that parents also adopt these magnificent values in all their interactions with everyone, including their children. Leading by example is the most effective way of *Tarbiyah* as unanimously agreed upon by the scholars.

---

39. (Q74, V38)
40. Agreed upon
41. Abu Dawood and At Termethy

Providing healthy and suitable alternatives

It is the responsibility of parents to find proper recreational alternatives to fill the lives of their children in western society, and to replace the bad influence of certain destructive social habits and of television. When the prophet SAAW came to Madinah, he found that they had two days of celebration and feasts. He told them Allah had replaced these two days for them with two better days; the two *Eids*, *Eid ul Adhha* and *Eidul Fitr*. You see, to change certain bad habits, the prophet SAAW didn't just order Muslims to stop these habits, rather he found a better alternative for them to fill the void which would result from stopping the old habits.

Rather than leaving our teens to spend lots of time in front of the television, or surfing the Internet, providing an educational entertaining Islamic video could be a good alternative. Even better than just watching Islamic videos, Muslim parents should strive to provide an active life style for their youth at the home level, at the community level, as well as at a societal level. This will help in filling their time with useful, productive, and entertaining activities. At home, they should be part of whatever is going on such as preparing meals, rearranging furniture, painting, landscaping, mowing the lawn, planning for a trip with the family, and so on. At the community level, parents should allow and facilitate for their teens to be involved in various activities such as planning and organizing events, being part of various committees, and so on.[42] Parents should also allow their teens to participate in certain mainstream programs to help in developing their skills. It is of utmost importance that parents work with their youth to find out the proper (healthy and clean) mainstream programs that they can participate in. This is an educational process and will help in developing teens' skills in decision-making, as well as strengthening their relationship with their parents.

---

42. See the section on "community role" for more detailed account of what the community can do to facilitate youth involvement and help in reducing teens rebellion

Solutions

BEING CONSISTENT

Various Qura'nic commandments were not just revealed once; they were repeated and emphasized over and over again in various ways. This indicates the importance of following up. Also, we read in Qura'n, "and enjoin thy people with prayer and be constant on it."[43] Again, this shows the importance of being consistent and repeating the same orders.

It is important for parents to observe this principle. When you instruct your child to do something, even something little, be serious, assertive and make sure you make eye contact with the child. If the child does not carry out the instruction, repeat the instruction again in a firm and serious voice but never lose your temper or shout.

When you say it only once and the child doesn't do it, ignoring this has serious consequences. From then on, the child will always take your instructions lightly. However, if you follow up on your instructions, the child will understand that you mean business, and that they are not a joke and will take them seriously.

This principle applies to every instruction and every interaction between you and your teen.

Many parents ignore the importance of being consistent in the training process. They apply rules sometime and ignore them other times. This may well leave the teen with the wrong impression and make him/her take his parents' instructions lightly. Next time the parents want to apply any disciplinary measure with the teen, he/she will tend to rebel against their instruction and may feel that it is too much. This is mainly because parents are not consistent in applying rules.

PROVIDING A HEALTHY, PLEASANT, LOVING AND POSITIVE FAMILY ATMOSPHERE

According to psychologists and scholars of child development, family atmosphere is one of the most crucial factors affecting the formation of

---

43. (Q20, V132)

children's personalities. While a positive and healthy family atmosphere helps in building a strong and loving bond between children and their parents, a negative and tense atmosphere has the opposite effect of straining the relationship between parents and their teens.[44] A pleasant family atmosphere, no doubt, contributes positively to reducing friction and confrontation between parents and teens. Teens feel more secure in their relationship with parents in this kind of family atmosphere. It also makes it easier for teens to approach their parents with most of their problems and solicit their advice in finding solutions for these problems. This in turn aids in avoiding cumulative negative feelings on the part of teens towards their parents, which will certainly lead to reducing teen rebellion.

WORK WITH YOUR TEEN TOWARD A COMMON POINT OF REFERENCE

When people have different sources to derive their principles from, they adopt various ways and have diverse perceptions of life. The majority of Muslim parents living in North America are immigrants. Their values and principles are mainly based on the traditions of their home countries and on the principles of Islam. On the other hand, teens who are born in North America, or who came with their families at very young age, will certainly have a different point of reference without a deliberate effort on the part of their parents to make them familiar with Islamic values. These teens' reference is mainly related to popular teen culture, which is almost completely opposite to Islamic values.

As such, if our children are left without being properly directed to the right sources in the most appealing and attractive way, they will end up adopting the mainstream pop culture as their point of reference. To ensure a common point of reference, parents have to work with their

---

44. See chapter 2 of *"Meeting the Challenge of Parenting in the West, an Islamic Perspective"* By Drs. Ekram and Mohamed R Beshir, amana Publications, third edition, 2004.

children from an early age to make them realize that proper understanding of Qur'an and the teachings of Prophet Muhammad SAAW are the only true and useful points of reference that Muslims should aspire to adopt and adhere to. This could be achieved by having an open channel of communication between parents and teens, and by discussing, dialoguing, and studying together the Qur'an and the teachings of Prophet Muhammad SAAW from an early age in a way that is relevant to the children's life and environment. It is not enough for parents to make their children memorize as many chapters of Qur'an and as many saying of the messenger SAAW as they can. But it is of great and immense importance that parents help their children understand what they memorize and let them know the implications of these teachings on their life in North America. Again, an open channel of communication and a focus on quality rather than quantity, as well as touching the children's hearts and souls, are very important. These are all key elements in bringing children closer to these teachings and making them willing to adopt them as their way of life, rather than succumbing to the popular teen culture as their point of reference.

HELP IN PROVIDING POSITIVE PEER PRESSURE

Teens are at a stage of their lives where the approval of their peers means a lot to them. If parents manage to surround their teen with a group of friends who share the same values, those friends will certainly apply positive peer pressure on the teen. They will also help in supporting each other and sheltering each other from the negative effects of mainstream youth. For Muslims living in North America or the West in general, this is not necessarily easy. Muslims are a minority and they live in scattered cities across the continent. Even those Muslims who live in large cities where the number of Muslims is considered sizable are not living in the same localities. This, no doubt requires extra effort on the parents' part to drive their teen around and make sure he/she hangs out with the right crowd and receives the needed support through positive peer pressure.

COMMUNITY LEVEL:

INTRODUCTION

At the community level, there are many things that can be done to help safeguard our Muslim youth and provide them with an alternative and positive environment in which they can feel they belong.

There is no doubt that Muslim communities have a great role to play in reducing teen rebellion and directing their energy to useful projects that could be of great benefit not only to the Muslim community, but also to the whole North American society. As they say, it takes a village to raise a child. Parents can do many things, but certain projects require the cooperation of many parents and others even need to be planned, designed, and executed by communities as a whole represented in local Islamic centers and even national Islamic institutions. As such, it is of utmost importance that all Muslim families not only support their local Islamic centers, but also contribute to the well being and strength of our National and North American Islamic organizations. The contribution of families and individuals shouldn't only be limited to financial support and monetary donations to these centers and organizations, but also through volunteering to help in various projects in any areas of expertise a person may posses. As Muslims, we must pull together, cooperate with each other and work together for the sake of our children. It is integral that Muslim teens have a strong Muslim community backing them up as a source of support, especially since they may not always feel a sense of belonging to mainstream society (and rightly so). So in the next section we will try to provide some suggestions for what can be done at the community level to help curb Muslim teen rebellion.

Solutions

SPECIFIC PROJECTS AND SUGGESTIONS

The following is a list of projects and suggestions that we think could be easily executed with reasonable efforts in any mid sized to large sized community. Some communities in various major cities in North America already have planned and executed some of these projects and they are successfully operating them and reaping the benefits for their teens. Of course the list we are providing here is not an exhaustive one and each community can think of more projects that may be suitable to their specific needs in this area:

Firstly, we need to establish youth centers. And of course, youth centers would be pointless if the youth don't come to them so we must strive very hard to both make the youth feel welcome in these centers and all our Islamic institutions and to ensure that these centers contain enough activities for children and youth that will draw them there. One way of making the youth feel more comfortable and welcome in our centers is to ensure youth representation on the board of these Islamic centers. By having representation from the youth on these boards, the youth will have a say in the way the centre is run or what events are held and this should subsequently lead to more youth involvement and participation when the youth find that the centre is relevant to them. Youth representation will also help cut the guess-work out of how the youth can be helped as the youth representatives will be able to voice the needs and concerns of the youth that need to be addressed.

The Muslim community needs to organize regular events that will engage the youth in a variety of activities. For example, they can hold regular youth camps that include both educational and recreational components. Sports tournaments or ski trips are also a great way for Muslim youth to bond with each other and participate in physical activity. The community can also pool their resources together to help in sponsoring youth to go on trips to attend regional conferences, national conventions or to perform Umrah.

Another responsibility that falls on the shoulders of the community in protecting Muslim youth from rebellion is the responsibility of creating awareness about this problem. If the community educates its members about the issue of teen rebellion and strives to find solutions for it, then this problem will decrease significantly. Here are some suggestions for initiatives that can be taken at the community level to address this issue:

• Support national organizations, particularly those that work in the family and youth area

• Actively educate community members about the importance of proper interaction with youth in our mosques and Islamic centers and the seriousness of not accommodating them in our institutions

• Sponsor developing parenting courses and encourage couples who are seeking marriage licenses to attend

• Sponsor regional and national conferences on the topic of Islamic parenting and invite scholars to present practical solutions to the problem

• Hold regular (Quarterly or bi-annually) local workshops on the topic and facilitate community members' attendance

• Follow up on these workshops by holding weekly or bi-weekly group discussions where attendees would study together a chapter of a proven good book on the subject

• Establish a library of good books and audiovisual materials on the subject

• Establish scholarships to create resource persons in the area. These scholarships will help community members excel in the area of social service and how to deal with youth

• Encourage youth to volunteer and participate in mainstream activities and projects (in a structured and organized fashion) such as:

– Blood donation clinics (blood drives)

– Shelters

Solutions

– Food banks
– Hospitals
– Planting trees
– Cleaning parks
– Information booths
– Political parties
– Snow Suit drives
– Etc.

Final Thoughts

In conclusion, we now see that rebellion among teens is normal and expected behaviour due to the nature of the adolescent stage as well as various other factors. Muslim teens are not excluded; in fact, there are added factors to make them rebel more than their peers. Fortunately, prophetic examples provide parents and community alike with wonderful guidelines to follow as a basis for developing comprehensive solutions to this problem. Parents can play a great role in reducing Muslim teen rebellion through the proper understanding of Islamic parenting methods as well as through following the great examples provided to us by Prophet Mohammad SAAW in dealing with this age group. The Muslim community can also play a pivotal role in reducing the severity of the problem, if not eradicating it fully.

In addition to the material provided in the previous chapters of this book, we would like to emphasize that when dealing with the teens in our lives, whether they are our own children or children in our community, we should try to keep these points in mind:

- If we want to change our children then we must change ourselves first
- Children become the attributes we give them.
- One of the major problems of Muslims living in the west in general is, in wanting to give our children what we did not have, we have forgotten to give them what we had.
- The louder we talk the quicker our children switch off.
- Discipline changes behaviour while punishment suppresses behaviour.
- Before applying any punishment to our children we should remember that the spectrum of Islamic discipline is very comprehensive and wide. Punishment only occupies the last one percent of it. As such, only resort to punishment, after trying other Prophetic disciplinary measures first. It works and it provides wonderful results.

Final Thoughts

- Manage your anger - anger is one letter away from danger

Our hope insha'a Allah, is that with the knowledge we presented in this short book, parents can renew their intention of raising their children as a way to worship Allah SWT and try to use the knowledge that Allah has blessed them with in the best way possible insha'a Allah. We ask Allah the Almighty to help us implement what we have learned and to make our children among the righteous.

Ameen.

References

————. *The Noble Qur'an, English Translation of the Meanings and Commentary.* Medina, Kingdom of Saudi Arabia: King Fahd Complex for the Printing of the Holy Qur'an, 1417 A.H.

Beshir, Dr. Ekram and Mohamed Rida Beshir. *Meeting the Challenge of Parenting in the West, An Islamic Perspective*, second edition. Beltsville, Maryland: amana publications, 2000.

Beshir, Dr. Ekram and Mohamed Rida Beshir. *Muslim Teens: Today's Worry, Tomorrow's Hope,* first edition. Beltsville, Maryland: amana publications, 2001.

Beshir, Drs. Ekram & Mohamed Rida Beshir. *"Answers to Frequently Asked Questions on Parenting,"* Part 1, Beltsville, Maryland: amana publications, 2005.

Beshir, Drs. Ekram & Mohamed Rida Beshir. *"Answers to Frequently Asked Questions on Parenting,"* Part 2, Beltsville, Maryland: amana publications, 2007

Imam Abi Al-Husain Muslim Ibn Al-Haggag Al-Qushairee Al-Naisabouree *Sahih Muslim*, first edition, Cairo: Dar Ihiaa' Alkutob Alarabia , 1955.

Imam Abi Abdellah Muhammad Ibn Ismail Ibn Ibraheem Ibn Al-Mogheirah Ibn Bardezabah Al-Bukhari, *Sahih al-Bukhari*,Cairo, Dar Al Shaa'b.

Imam Al-Hafez Abi Dawud Sulaiman Ibn Al-Asha'th Al-Sagestany Al-Azdei *Sunan Aby Dawud*, first edition, Bayroot, Dar Ibn Hazm , 1998.

References

Imam Al-Hafez Aby Abderahaman Ahmad Ibn Shua'ib Ibn Ali Ibn Senan Ibn Dinar Al-Nisa'i *Sunan Al-Nisa'i*, first edition, Bayroot, Dar Ibn Hazm, 1999.

Imam Ibn Majah Sunan Ibn Majah, first edition, Cairo, *Dar Ihiaa'At Turath Al-A'raby*, 1975

Imam Malek Ibn Anas, Mowata' Al Imam Malek, Ninth edition, Bayroot, *Dar Al-Nafae's* , 1985, Prepared by *Ahmad Rateb Armoosh*

Other books of Hadith, *"Ahmad, Tabarani, Tirmidhi,..."*

Mohammad Gawad, Al-Imama Ali encyclopedia, Volume 1, *Dar Al-Tayar Al-Jadded*

Shaykh Muhammad Al-Ghazaly, *Muslim Character*, first edition, Salimiah, Kuwait, International Islamic Federation of Student Organizations, 1983

Shaykh Abdul Fattah Abu Ghudda, *Islamic manners,* Swansea, U.K., Awakening Publications, 2001